IMPRESSIONS *of*

IRELAND

Picture Acknowledgements

All photographs are held in the Automobile Association's own photo library (AA World Travel Library) and were taken by the following photographers:

Liam Blake 59; Jamie Blandford 9, 34, 37, 43, 46, 47; Chris Coe 3, 73, 77, 88; Ian Dawson 29, 39, 80, 82, 83, 86, 90; Steve Day 7, 20, 27, 32, 36, 49, 51, 54, 62, 65, 69, 74, 79, 81, 85, 87, 91, 93; Michael Diggin 24, 25, 26; Slide File 16; Derek Forss 18, 52, 75, 94; Chris Hill 23, 28, 30; Stephen Hill 5, 8, 14, 31, 35, 44, 61; Caroline Jones 12, 20, 38, 55, 57, 66, 67, 78, 92; T King 71; Simon McBride 13, 17, 19, 21, 50, 58, 64, 70; George Munday 11, 40, 41, 53, 56, 89; Michael Short 10, 45, 63, 72, 84; Wyn Voysey 48; Stephen Whitehorn 33, 42, 60, 76, 95; Peter Zollier 15.

Opposite: Celtic crosses on Inishmore, the largest of the Aran Islands.

INTRODUCTION

It's impossible to separate Ireland from the image of the legendary 40 shades of green that make up this Emerald Isle. You may have to put up with the unpredictable showers of its maritime climate, but your reward is the dazzling spectrum of colour on the lush pastures and rolling hills when the sun breaks through.

This island's landscape is surprisingly varied, given its size. Much of the rugged coastline is backed by a rim of bare mountains and dramatic sea cliffs, with the basalt organ-pipe columns of the northern coastline contrasting with the sandy bays of the southwest. A limestone plain spreads across the interior, most famously exposed in the crevassed, flower-strewn rocky plain of the Burren. Further inland the terrain ranges from flat, lush pastureland to rolling green hills, threaded by silvery winding rivers and dotted with lakeland regions. The ancient oak forests are long gone, but their legacy may be seen in the still vast stretches of damp peat bog in the central and northwestern regions, part of a valuable and unique ecosystem.

Ireland's winding country roads and beautiful scenery demand a leisurely pace. Besides — and despite the modern reputation of the thrusting Celtic Tiger economy — it's almost a sacrilege to hurry here. On any journey of discovery, you should take time to chat with the locals, linger in the brightly painted coastal towns or vibrant cities, share a story or a song in a local pub.

The country's rich heritage stretches back to prehistoric times, and early history is surprisingly visible. Megalithic tombs, cairns and stone circles are scattered throughout the countryside, testimony to an ancient and mysterious race. Alongside remnants of primitive dwellings, such as ring forts and crannógs (artificial islands built on lakes), they lend a distinctive sense of wonder and timelessness to the landscape. Ireland has been known as the cradle of Roman Catholic Christianity in the West since the advent of St Patrick in 5th century, and the early Christian era gave the country some of its most striking architecture. The slender round towers, unique to the island, and tall, elaborately carved high crosses are key features of monastic sites around the country such as Glendalough and Clonmacnoise. Most of Ireland's 2,500 castles and fortified tower houses date from the late 12th to the 16th centuries and are in the west and southwest. During the 1700s and early 1800s the aristocracy built splendid neoclassical mansions such as Castle Coole and Bunratty House, and Dublin acquired the elegant Georgian squares for which it is famous.

Impressions of Ireland takes a leisurely look through the photographer's lens at the places and people that make this island so special. It explores the whole of it — both the province of Northern Ireland and the independent Republic of the south, which together form a special green corner of the British Isles.

Murals adorn a shop front in Kinvarra, County Galway.

Ladies' View, in Killarney National Park, was so named because it was particularly admired by
Queen Victoria's ladies-in-waiting during a visit in 1861.
Opposite: the Burren, a limestone plateau south of Galway in County Clare.

Some of the remains at Glendalough, a monastic site in the Wicklow Mountains.

Mussenden Temple was built as a library in the 18th century by the Bishop of Derry, on the Downhill Estate in the northwest.

The Gallarus Oratory, an early Christian church dating from AD800, on the Dingle Peninsula.
Opposite: a view towards Blarney Castle, northwest of Cork. Its Stone of Eloquence is believed to bestow the
'gift of the gab' on all those who kiss it.

One of the many Celtic crosses erected as memorials to islanders who died overseas or at sea, on the island of Inishmore, largest of the Aran Islands in Galway Bay.

The rocky upland of the Burren is known for its rich flora consisting of both alpine and Mediterranean species.

The barrel-vaulted Long Room of the library at Trinity College, Dublin. It houses more than 200,000 of Ireland's most important books, manuscripts and historical documents.

Traditional Irish step dancing (or Irish dance) at the Galway International Oyster Festival.

Mount Errisbeg, near Roundstone in Connemara.
Opposite: the medieval buildings on top of the Rock of Cashel, County Tipperary.

The Lower Lake at Glendalough (which means 'two lakes'), in the Wicklow Mountains.

Trinity College in Dublin was founded in 1592, but most of the buildings are 18th and 19th century.

The 3-mile-long (5km) Back Strand at the resort of Tramore, in County Waterford. It has been attracting holidaymakers ever since wealthy Waterford merchant Batholomew Rivers transformed the former fishing village in 1785.

Parke's Castle, on the edge of Lough Gill in County Leitrim. The interior of the castle has been restored using Irish oak timber and traditional methods of craftsmanship.

The cliffs of Fair Head on Ballycastle Bay, County Antrim. In 1898 Marconi sent the world's first underwater telecommunication from here across the sound to Rathlin Island.

The memorial tower to the 3rd Marquis of Londonderry in Scrabo Country Park, near Newtownards in County Down.

Baurtregaum, whose Gaelic name means 'top of the three corries', in the Slieve Mish Mountain Range.

The Record Tower — the largest visible fragment of Dublin's original Norman castle — served as a high security prison and held Irish hostages and priests in Tudor times.

The beauty of Lough Key, County Roscommon, has inspired many legends about love and death.

The Slieve League (Grey Mountain) cliffs on the west coast of Donegal are among the highest in Europe.

Lough Gill, County Sligo, is the location of the Lake Isle of Innisfree, made famous by the poet W. B. Yeats.
Opposite: the estuary of the Blackwater River, close to the town of Youghal on the Cork coast.

The ruins of Temple Jarlath in the Galway town of Tuam. According to legend, St Jarlath took a broken chariot wheel as a sign to found his monastic settlement here in the 6th century.

The copper-topped rotunda of the Four Courts, completed in 1796, overlooks the River Liffey in Dublin.

Inchydoney Island, west of Cork, was joined to the mainland by two causeways in the 19th century.

Baltimore Beacon (also known as 'Lot's Wife', because it resembles a pillar of salt), in County Cork. It was part of a series of lighthouses and beacons dotted around the Irish coast to form a warning system.

The hill of Uisneagh in County Westmeath, said to be the meeting point of the five ancient provinces of Ireland. It was also the seat of the High Kings of Ireland for 200 years.

Gougane Barra Lake in County Cork. The island is where St Finbarr, patron saint of Cork, founded his hermitage in the 6th century (the chapel shown dates from the 19th century).

Stormont Castle, in Belfast, is the seat of the Northern Ireland Assembly. In 1858 the architect Thomas Turner
turned the original plain Georgian house into the battlemented and turreted baronial castle we see today.
Opposite: the Lower Lake at Glendalough.

Mount Stewart House in County Down has one of the finest gardens in Ireland, with many rare plants.
It was largely created by Lady Londonderry, wife of the 7th Marquess, in the 1920s.

The Carrick-a-Rede rope bridge on the North Antrim coast: not for the faint hearted.

Much of Dublin's architecture dates from the 18th and 19th centuries, when the city grew and prospered.

View of Derrynane from the Ring of Kerry, the road that hugs the Iveragh Peninsula in County Kerry.

43

Jerpoint Abbey, near Thomastown in County Kilkenny, was built around 1160 by the King of Ossory, Donal MacGillapatrick, for the Benedictine monks.
Opposite: the Cliffs of Moher, bordering the Burren in County Clare.

Located at the base of Mount Eagle on the Dingle peninsula is the 10th-century Dunbeg drystone fort.

Dunmanus Bay and the Sheep's Head Peninsula in the southwest corner of County Cork.

The base of the monument to Daniel O'Connell in O'Connell Street, Dublin.
O'Connell (1785–1847) was known as the 'Liberator' for his campaign to have anti-Catholic legislation
repealed by the British Government.

The more rugged face of Tramore. Waterford's premier resort is better known for its huge sandy beach.

The Poulnabrone portal tomb at the heart of the Burren, County Clare. Its name means 'hole of the sorrows', and during excavations in the 1980s the uncremated remains of up to 20 bodies were found.

Detail of Dublin's neoclassical City Hall, which now houses a multimedia exhibition of city events.

Glenarm, the most southerly of the nine Glens of Antrim. The village, where the river meets the sea, claims to be the oldest town in Ireland after being granted a charter in the 12th century.

The circular stone fort of Grianan of Aileach, near Letterkenny in County Donegal. Within the walls are small chambers and a series of stairs at regular intervals that give access to the wall-walk.

Leenane, at the head of Killary Harbour, is described as the 'gateway to Connemara'. The 16-km (10-mile) inlet is known as Ireland's only fiord, though whether it was formed by glaciers is disputed.

Pádraic Pearse's Cottage in Connemara. Pearse (1879–1916), poet and leader of the 1916 Easter uprising, used it as a summer residence.

Glenveagh Castle on Lough Veagh, County Donegal.

A traditional folk band occupies a corner of the popular Sky and the Ground Pub, Wexford.

Aghadoe Hill, near Killarney in the far southwest.

Lough Conn in County Mayo. Connected to the sea by the River Moy, the lake is renowned for its salmon fishing.

The Government Buildings in Merrion Street Upper, Dublin.

Brandon Bay on the northern shores of the Dingle Peninsula, in County Kerry, is one of the top surfing beaches in the southwest.

The ruins of the 13th-century castle at Ferns, County Wexford.

Heathland near Sally Gap – Ireland's highest crossroads – in the Wicklow Mountains. The Gaelic name, of which the English is a corruption, means 'saddle', as in 'mountain pass'.

Gothic-revival Tullynally Castle at Castlepollard, County Westmeath.
Opposite: the grounds of Blarney Castle in County Cork, where ancient lime, oak, beech and gnarled
walnut trees create magical glades.

*St Kevin's Church, in Glendalough, is also known as St Kevin's Kitchen – possibly because of
the chimney-like tower.*

The Blasket Islands, 3 miles (5km) off the tip of the Dingle Peninsula, are Europe's most westerly point.

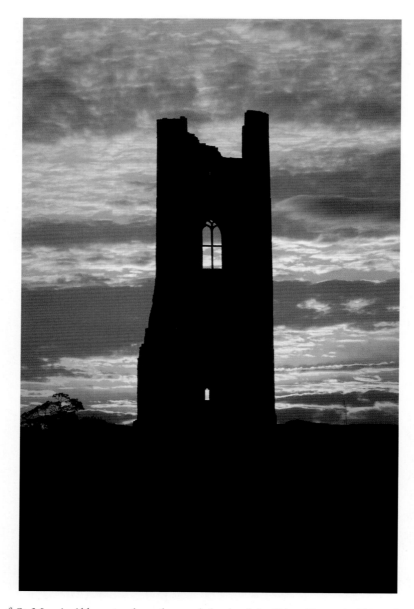

The ruins of St Mary's Abbey stand on the north bank of the River Boyne in Trim, County Meath.

Dublin's Custom House on the River Liffey. It was the first major public building to be built in the city.

A fishing fleet in Skerries Harbour, north of Dublin.
Opposite: the Old Head of Kinsale – a diamond-shaped promontory jutting into the Atlantic in County
Cork. A golf course is laid out on the top of it.

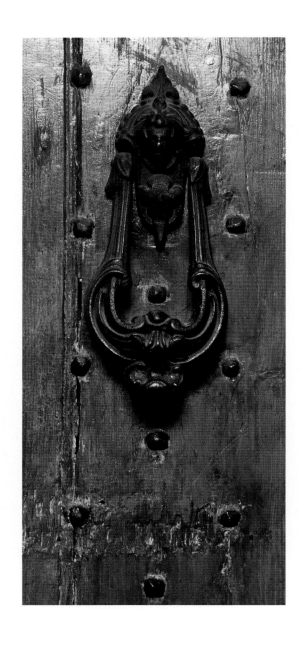

A door to Enniscorthy Castle, built by the Normans in the middle of the town of Enniscorthy and now home to the Wexford County Museum.

The monastic remains at Kilmacduagh, near Gort in County Galway. Round towers such as this one were built primarily as bell towers between the 9th and 12th centuries.

The ruins of Fethard Castle in County Wexford. In the 15th century an L-shaped fortified hall house was built around the gate tower of an even older castle.

The harbour at Kinsale, one of the most fashionable resorts on the southwest coast and a centre for yachting, sea angling and golf.

The 'Hands Across the Divide' statue, which joins Londonderry's Catholic and Protestant areas.
Opposite: Ha'Penny Bridge spanning the River Liffey in Dublin. Officially called Wellington Bridge after
the 'Iron Duke', it acquired its nickname from the toll paid to cross the river — one old half penny.

The Loughcrew Cairns, also known as the Hills of the Witch, in County Meath.

Millennium Walk, Dublin.

79

Carlingford Lough, a sea inlet on the east coast. The Mountains of Mourne lie to the north and the Cooley Mountains to the south.

*Kylemore Abbey, in the heart of Connemara. The former Benedictine abbey, now a girls' boarding school,
has a newly restored Victorian walled garden.*

The view from the Parliament Buildings, known as Stormont Castle, in Belfast. The statue commemorates Edward Carson (1854–1935), leader of the Irish Unionist Parliamentary Party.

Glenballyemon — one of the nine Glens of Antrim on the northeast coast. Table-topped Lurigethan Mountain to the right has long been associated with fairy legends and the 'wee folk'.

A country garage near the village of Wellington Bridge, at the head of the Bannow Bay Estuary, in County Wexford. The first Normans to reach Ireland are believed to have landed in the area.

Eden Quay, to the east of O'Connell Bridge, seen from Burgh Quay, Dublin.

Glendun, another of the nine Glens of Anrim. The mountain of Crocknacreeva and Gruig Top form one side and Crocknamoyle and Crockaneel the other.

View over Dublin. The neo-classical, green-domed Four Courts is a landmark of the city.

The ruins of Dunluce Castle stand on a 100ft-high (30-m) basalt stack on the North Antrim coast.
There is a sea cave underneath, which is accessible both by land and sea.

Mount Errigal, Donegals' highest mountain, with Dunlewy church, built from local white marble.

The quartzite cone of Mount Errigal's western flank.

The Bank of Ireland, which faces College Green in Dublin, was the original home of Irish Parliament.

A view of the scattered remains at Glendalough, in County Wicklow, the monastery founded by St Kevin in the 6th century.

Celebrations in Dublin on St Patrick's Day (17 March).

The beach at Youghal, a popular resort on the southeast coast of County Cork.

Sunset over the River Liffey, Dublin.

INDEX